S0-ACR-338

CHEROKEE

OCT 1 6 1990

Exploring Science

The Exploring Science series is designed to familiarize young students with science topics taught in grades 4–9. The topics in each book are divided into knowledge and understanding sections, followed by exploration by means of simple projects or experiments. The topics are also sequenced from easiest to more complex, and should be worked through until the correct level of attainment for the age and ability of the student is reached. Carefully planned Test Yourself questions at the end of each topic allow the student to gain a sense of achievement on mastering the subject.

EXPLORING
MAGNETS

Ed Catherall

STECK-VAUGHN
LIBRARY
Austin, Texas

Exploring Science

Electricity
Light
Magnets
Soil and Rocks
Sound
Weather

Cover illustrations:
Left *The magnetic field of a horseshoe magnet, shown by iron filings.*
Above right *A graphics picture of the magnetic field of the human body.*
Below right *A diagram showing how an electric current flows in a wire when the wire is moved in a magnetic field.*

Frontispiece *A button magnet is repelled by a disc of super-conducting material. This is an example of magnetic levitation.*

Editor: Elizabeth Spiers
Editor, American Edition: Susan Wilson
Series designer: Ross George
Designer: Jenny Searle

Published in the United States in 1990 by Steck-Vaughn Co., Austin, Texas, a subsidiary of National Education Corporation.

First published in 1989 by
Wayland (Publishers) Ltd

©Copyright 1989 Wayland (Publishers) Ltd

Library of Congress Cataloging-in-Publication Data

Catherall, Ed.
  Exploring Magnets / Ed Catherall.
    p.   cm — (Exploring science)
  Includes bibliographical references.
  Summary: Discusses what magnets are and how they work, describes the properties of magnets, and includes projects and activities, such as making a magnetic race track and a magnetic compass.
    ISBN 0-8114-2593-2
    1. Magnets—Juvenile literature.   2. Magnets—Experiments--Juvenile literature. [1. Magnets.   2. Magnets—Experiments.
3. Experiments.]   I. Title.   II. Series: Catherall, Ed.   Exploring science.
QC757.5.C37   1990   89-26116
538'.4—dc20   CIP
                                                        AC
Typeset by Multifacit Graphics
Printed in Italy by G. Canale of C.S.p.A., Turin
Bound in the United States by Lake Book, Melrose Park, IL
1 2 3 4 5 6 7 8 9 0 Ca 94 93 92 91 90

Contents

WHAT IS A MAGNET?

A magnet is a piece of metal, ore, or stone that has the power to attract or repel (push away) certain materials. Magnets occur naturally in the ground. Lodestone, which has been mined for centuries, is a magnetic stone made of iron ore. Many thousands of years ago, the Chinese explored the magnetic properties of lodestone.

Today, magnets are made of different substances and are found in a range of shapes. The most common shapes are bar, horseshoe, button, and ring. A horseshoe magnet is really a bar magnet that has been bent into a horseshoe shape.

Right *A piece of lodestone.*

Below *Weakly magnetic household stickers.*

Magnets come in different sizes and strengths. Some are small and weak, such as those found on the backs of stickers that are put on refrigerator doors. Others are large and strong, and can be used to lift cars and sort scrap iron.

ACTIVITIES

> **YOU NEED**
>
> - **magnets of different shapes**
> - **a smooth piece of paper**
> - **a ruler**
> - **a pin**

THE SHAPE OF MAGNETS

1 Collect magnets of different shapes.
2 Sort them into bar, horseshoe, button, and ring shapes.
3 Which magnets have a keeper?
4 Draw around some of the magnets.

GOING ON A MAGNET SEARCH

1 Look at home, at school, in toy stores, supermarkets, and hardware stores for things that use magnets.
2 Write down how the magnets are used and what shape they are.

THE STRENGTH OF YOUR MAGNETS

1 Test the strength of your magnets. One way of doing this is to lay a pin on a smooth sheet of paper.
2 Put a ruler down beside the pin.
3 Slide your magnet along the edge of the ruler, toward the pin.
4 When the pin starts to move toward the magnet, measure how far it is between the magnet and the pin.

5 The closer you have to move your magnet, the weaker it is.
6 Put your magnets into three groups: strong, medium, and weak.
7 Which is the strongest magnet?
8 What shape is it?
9 When you have finished using the magnets, replace their keepers and store them carefully.

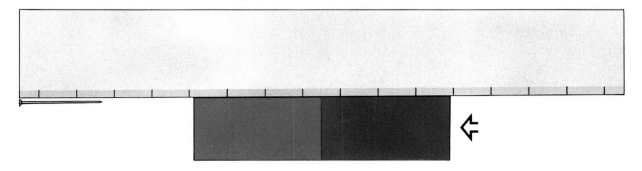

> ## TEST YOURSELF
>
> 1. What is a magnet?
> 2. Name three shapes of magnets.
> 3. List three ways in which magnets are used.

WHAT WILL A MAGNET ATTRACT?

The Eiffel Tower in Paris, France. This incredible building has stood for 100 years. It is made completely from steel, which is strengthened iron. Pure iron would be too soft to support this building.

A magnet attracts magnetic materials with a force called magnetism. There are different kinds of magnetic materials. The most common is iron. All objects made of iron are magnetic. The most magnetic is pure iron, which is a very soft metal that is rarely used for building or making objects. The iron that we use has been strengthened or hardened. Iron can be strengthened by adding other substances to it. Most of these other materials are not magnetic, so they dilute (make weaker) the magnetism in the iron. As iron is made stronger to become steel, it becomes less magnetic. However, even the hardest steel has enough iron in it to be magnetic.

Sometimes iron and steel are thinly coated with other, nonmagnetic materials. Iron can be coated with metals such as tin or zinc, or with paints and plastics. This stops the iron or steel from rusting. Provided there is plenty of iron present, magnetic force penetrates the coating. A "tin" can is iron coated with tin and so is magnetic, as you will investigate in the next chapter.

There are a few other metals that are magnetic. One such metal is pure nickel. In most countries, the coins that are not worth very much have some nickel in them. Coins made from a copper-nickel alloy contain only a very small amount of nickel. This is not enough to be attracted to the kind of magnet that you would use. The metal cobalt is also magnetic.

ACTIVITY

> YOU NEED
>
> - **a strong magnet**
> - **a variety of objects to be tested—include wood, rubber, plastics, and different metals**

1 Sort your objects into two sets:
Set 1: things you think a magnet will attract.
Set 2: things you think a magnet will not attract.

Things I think a magnet will attract	True or false?
paper clip	
coin	
aluminum foil	
Things I think a magnet will not attract	True or false?
cotton	
pencil	
plastic ruler	

2 Now test each object, one at a time, with your magnet.

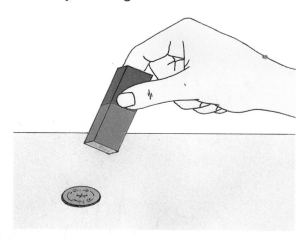

3 Record in one list all the objects that were not attracted.
4 Record in another list all the objects that were attracted.
5 What are all these objects made of? You may need to ask your teacher about some of the metals.
6 Were your guesses correct? Were there any surprises?

TEST YOURSELF

1. Name two metals that are magnetic.
2. Name three things that you would not expect to be magnetic.
3. Which substance is more magnetic—pure iron or steel? Why?

MAGNETIC STRENGTH

The ends of a bar magnet attract iron filings, which are magnetic. The stronger the magnet, the more iron filings it will attract.

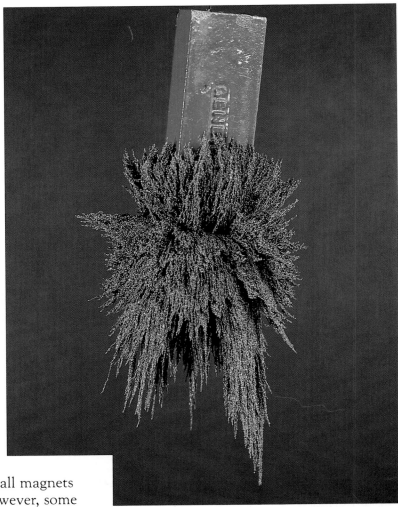

You have already learned that all magnets attract magnetic materials. However, some parts of a magnet are stronger than others. In order to find out where a magnet's strength is, we have to find a way of measuring the magnetic pull, or force of attraction. If you hold a magnetic material near a very strong magnet, you can feel this force pulling the material toward the magnet. With weak magnets, it is more difficult to feel this force or to measure it. One of the ways of measuring this force of attraction is to see how much force is needed to pull the magnetic material away from the magnet. The amount of force needed to pull the material away equals the force that holds the material to the magnet.

It is not easy to compare the strengths of magnets of different shapes. A big magnet is not necessarily stronger than a small one. A scientific test must be fair. So to compare magnets, you must always use magnets of the same shape. You can use the same test to find out where a magnet has its strongest part or parts.

ACTIVITY

WHERE IS A BAR MAGNET'S STRENGTH?

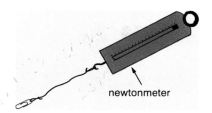

newtonmeter

YOU NEED

- **a ruler**
- **a long, strong bar magnet**
- **a pencil**
- **small paper clips**
- **thread**
- **a newtonmeter (or spring balance)**

6 See how many paper clips you can hang from the end.

15 Ask a friend to hold the magnet to the table.
16 Place the paper clip on one of the marks on the magnet and pull the newtonmeter.
17 On your newtonmeter read the force needed to pull the paper clip off the magnet.

1 Measure the length of the bar magnet.
2 Use a pencil to mark the middle.
3 Divide each half into 4 equal parts.
4 Mark each of these parts with a pencil.

7 Take the paper clips off.
8 Repeat your test at each of the marks and at the other end.
9 Record your results as a diagram.
10 Where on the magnet could you hang the most clips?
11 Which is the strongest part of a magnet?
12 Repeat this experiment using another bar magnet. Are your results the same?
13 Use the first bar magnet again.
14 Using thread, tie one paper clip to the newtonmeter.

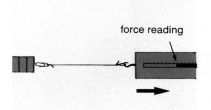

force reading

18 Repeat your test at each of the marks on the magnet and at both ends.
19 At which point on your magnet is the most force needed to pull off the paper clip?
20 Are your results the same as before?

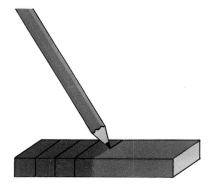

5 Start at one end of the magnet.

To find out more about this, see page 32.

TEST YOURSELF

1. If you hold a magnetic material near a strong magnet, what can you feel?
2. Where is the strongest and the weakest magnetic pull in a bar magnet?

MAGNETS ACT THROUGH THINGS

You know that magnets give out an invisible magnetic force called magnetism. You also know, from your experiments on page 11, that the ends of a bar magnet have the most magnetism. The magnetic force from a very strong magnet will attract objects over a considerable distance.

Many substances are not attracted to magnets. You have found this out from the activity on page 9. Air is not magnetic. The magnetic force streams out of the end of a bar magnet and passes through air to attract a magnetic object.

A magnetic drawing set. A special "pencil" can be moved over the screen, and iron filings underneath are attracted to the magnet on the end of the pencil.

PERMANENT MAGNETIC PENCIL

DIRECTIONS ON BACK of CARD

$3 \times 1 = 3$
$3 \times 2 = 9$
$3 \times 3 = 9$
$3 \times 4 = 12$
$= 15$
$6 = 18$

Things that are not magnetic, like air, allow the force of magnetism to pass through them. This force will continue to attract a magnetic substance on the other side. Remember that the distance away from a magnet is important (see page 7). If you place a magnetic object on the other side of a thick nonmagnetic substance, the object may be too far away from the magnet to be attracted to it.

ACTIVITY

> ### YOU NEED
>
> - **a strong bar magnet**
> - **paper clips**
> - **sheets of plastic, paper, cloth, rubber, foil**
> - **a plastic beaker**
> - **a glass jar**
> - **a cup**
> - **water**

1 Wrap the magnet in a sheet of plastic. Can it attract a paper clip?

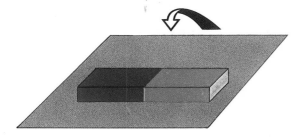

2 Wrap the magnet in each sheet one at a time. Does the magnetism pass through each sheet?

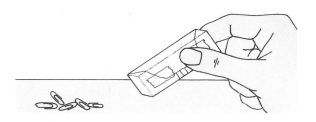

3 Put the paper clip into a beaker.
4 Can you lift the clip up the side, using a magnet outside the beaker?

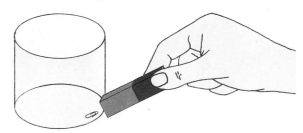

5 Repeat this experiment using the cup, then the jar.
6 Fill the beaker with water. Will magnetism work through water?
7 Try all kinds of different materials. Record the results.
8 Is there anything that a magnet will not work through?

TEST YOURSELF

1. Is air magnetic?
2. Where does most magnetic force leave a bar magnet?
3. Name four things that are not magnetic.

MAGNETIC SHIELDS

The magnetic field of this bar magnet is shown by iron filings scattered on a thin sheet of plastic lying over the magnet. The magnetic force is strongest at the ends, but can be felt all around the magnet.

You have seen that a bar magnet gives out most of its magnetic force from each of its ends. But this force also spreads in all directions along the magnet.

Like any type of force, magnetism is useful but can also be a nuisance. For example, a person working with a very strong magnet may be wearing a watch. Parts of that watch may be made of steel, which is magnetic. The magnetism from the strong magnet may affect the watch, slowing down the moving parts, or stopping them altogether. There may be other pieces of machinery nearby, made of steel. The strong magnet could interfere with their moving parts as well.

This effect can be controlled by using a magnetic shield. You know that magnetism works through most nonmagnetic materials, so a magnetic shield is made of a magnetic material. This picks up the magnetic force and spreads it out, so that the magnetic force is made much weaker and has a less damaging effect on nearby machines.

ACTIVITY

YOU NEED

- cellophane tape
- a strong bar magnet
- a ruler
- books
- a tack
- a wooden block
- a paper clip
- thread
- a tin can's lid
- a range of materials cut in circles the same size as the can lid
- pliers

1 Tape the bar magnet to the ruler.
2 Hold the ruler in a stack of books.
3 Tie a thread to a paper clip.
4 Check that the paper clip is pulled up by the magnet.
5 Push the tack into a wooden block.
6 Tie the thread to the tack so that the clip is pulled up by the magnet.

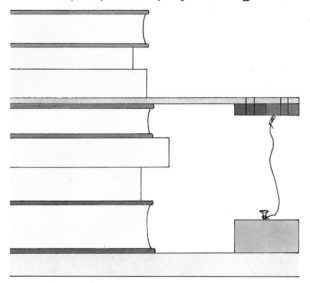

7 Hold the can lid with pliers and put it between the magnet and the paper clip. What happens?

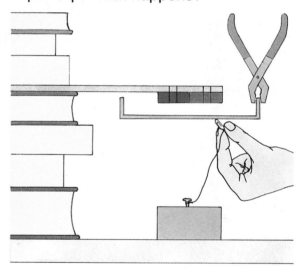

8 Is the lid acting as a magnetic shield?
9 Try using circles made of different materials.
10 Does the magnetic force act through them, or are they magnetic shields?

TEST YOURSELF

1. What materials make good magnetic shields?
2. Name three things that would not work as a magnetic shield.
3. Why are magnetic shields useful?

TEMPORARY MAGNETS

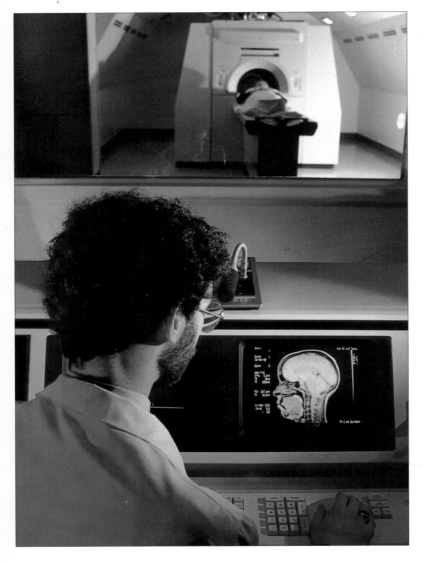

A brain scan made using nuclear magnetic resonance (NMR). The patient lies in a huge magnetic field. Returning signals are used to make a computer picture of the brain. NMR scans do not hurt the patient.

You know a magnet's force is all around it, although it is stronger in some places than in others. This surrounding force is called the magnetic field. As you move away from the magnet, the magnetic field gets weaker.

When you studied magnetic shields, you found out that magnetic materials, such as iron and nickel, can, if placed in a mag-netic field, absorb the magnetic force and so become magnets themselves. If the original magnet is taken away, a magnetic material loses most of its magnetic power and is no longer a magnet. The magnetic object was only a temporary magnet. It was a magnet only when placed near a strong magnet—that is, placed in a strong mag-netic field, as we will discuss on page 32.

ACTIVITY

MAKING A TEMPORARY MAGNET

YOU NEED

- **a strong bar magnet**
- **paper clips**
- **a steel screw**
- **a steel nail**
- **a brass screw**

1 Use your bar magnet to check that the paper clips are magnetic.

2 Hold the steel screw near a paper clip. Is the screw a magnet?

3 Do this with the nail and brass screw.

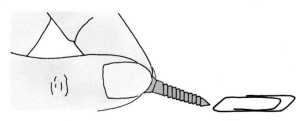

4 Put the head of the steel screw against the end of the magnet.

5 Does the screw now attract a paper clip? Is the screw magnetic?

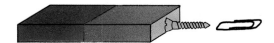

6 Slowly move the magnet away from the screw. What happens? Is the screw still magnetic?

7 Repeat this experiment using the steel nail and the brass screw.

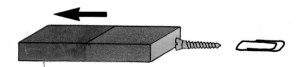

8 Place the paper clip on a table.

9 Make sure that the magnet does not touch the screw, but gets very close to it. Does the screw attract the clip?

10 Is the screw acting as a magnet?

11 Slowly remove the magnet. What happens to the screw?

12 Repeat this experiment using the steel nail and brass screw.

13 Record your results.

TEST YOURSELF

1. What is a magnetic field?
2. Name two objects that could be made into temporary magnets.
3. Why are temporary magnets so called?

PERMANENT MAGNETS

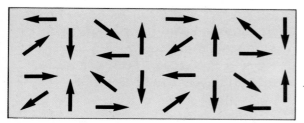

Magnetic material (unmagnetized)

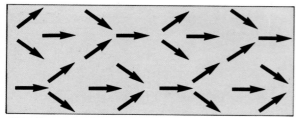

Weak magnet

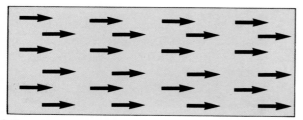

Strong magnet

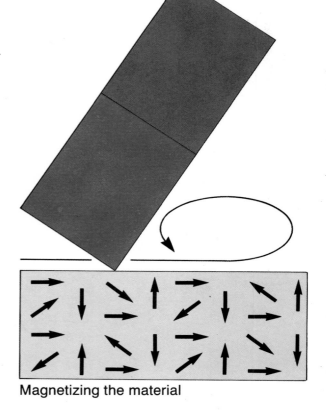

Magnetizing the material

A magnetic material, such as iron or nickel, can be thought of as consisting of millions of tiny magnets. They all face in different directions. A magnet, because it is a magnetic material, also consists of millions of tiny magnets. The difference between a magnet and a magnetic material is that all the tiny magnets are facing the same way in a magnet. In a bar magnet, all the tiny magnets face one end of the bar.

To make a permanent magnet from magnetic material, you have to line up the tiny magnets that are all facing in different directions. This can be done in several ways.

Individual particles in a magnetic material can be lined up by a magnet.

One way is by stroking the magnetic material with a magnet. With each stroke of the magnet, some of the little magnets get pulled into line. As you continue to stroke the piece of iron or nickel, more and more of the little magnets are lined up. This makes the magnetic material into a magnet. The more little magnets are in line, the stronger the magnet becomes. Of course, it should be possible to get all the little magnets in line, but it is very difficult.

ACTIVITY

MAKING A PERMANENT MAGNET

> **YOU NEED**
>
> - **a steel knitting needle or long steel nail**
> - **paper clips**
> - **a strong bar magnet**

1 Does the needle (or nail) attract a paper clip?
2 Is the needle magnetic?
3 Put the needle on the table.
4 Hold it with your fingers and stroke it 30 times with one end of the magnet.
5 Make sure that you always use the same end of the magnet.
6 Always stroke the needle in the same direction.

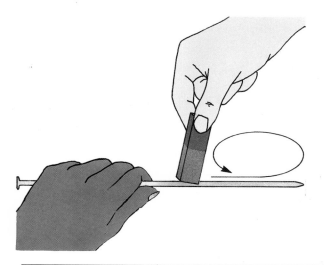

7 Does the needle pick up the paper clip now?
8 How many paper clips will it hold?
9 Stroke the needle another 30 times. Use the same end of the magnet and stroke in the same direction.
10 How many paper clips will the needle pick up now?
11 Is the needle more magnetic?

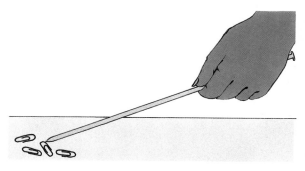

12 Repeat this experiment twice more, adding 30 strokes each time.
13 Record how many paper clips the needle will hold each time.

Total number of strokes to needle	How many paper clips will it hold?
30	
60	
90	

TEST YOURSELF

1. If the magnetic material consists of millions of tiny magnets, draw the difference between a magnetized and unmagnetized nail.
2. How can you make a length of iron into a magnet?

CARING FOR MAGNETS

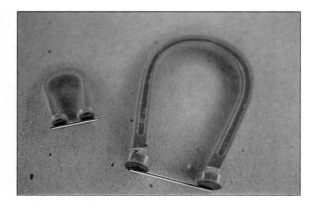

Horseshoe magnets with their keepers.

If a magnet consists of millions of tiny magnets all lined up facing the same way, they must stay lined up for the magnet to keep its power. Each time a magnet is knocked or dropped, a few of these little magnets jump out of line. This means there are fewer lined up, so the magnet is weaker. If you are very careless with it and knock it repeatedly, most of the tiny magnets jump out of line and it is no longer a magnet.

If a magnet is heated, the heat makes the little magnets move about. They jump out of line and the magnet loses its power.

Magnets have to be stored very carefully. Bar and horseshoe magnets should be stored with their soft iron keepers in place. Bar magnets should be stored in pairs with keepers at each end. They should be facing in opposite directions, so that they naturally stick together. Avoid storing many magnets close to each other, just in case one strong magnet is pulling the little magnets out of line inside the other magnets.

Remember: when you have finished using magnets, always put them away carefully, without hitting them. This way, magnets should last a long time.

ACTIVITIES

YOU NEED

- **a small test tube and cork**
- **iron filings**
- **paper clips**
- **a strong bar magnet**

1 Fill the test tube with iron filings.
2 Cork the tube to keep the filings in.

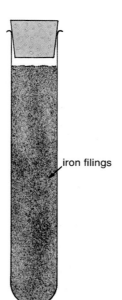

iron filings

3 Is the test tube magnetic? Check it with paper clips.
4 Stroke the tube 30 times with one end of a bar magnet, as you did on page 19.

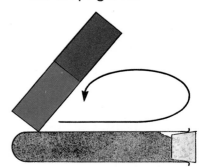

5 How many paper clips will your tube of iron filings pick up now?
6 Shake the test tube several times.
7 How many paper clips will it pick up now?
8 Can you shake all the magnetism out?

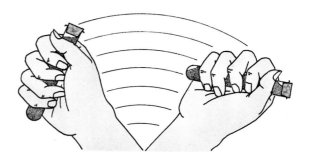

YOU NEED

• **a magnetized knitting needle (see page 19)**
• **a strong bar magnet**
• **paper clips**
• **a stone**
• **pliers**
• **a heat source**

1 How many paper clips will your magnetized needle pick up?
2 Hit the needle hard against a stone 10 times.

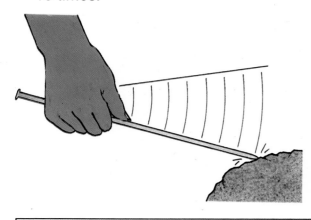

3 Test the strength of your knitting needle again.
4 What happened to the magnetism?
5 Can you hit all the magnetism out of the needle?
6 Remagnetize the needle (see page 19). Check its strength.
7 Using pliers, hold it in a flame.

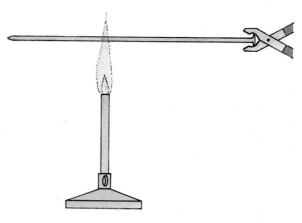

8 When the needle is cool, test its magnetism. Has it changed?

WARNING: Be very careful when heating things. Get an adult to help you.

TEST YOURSELF

1. What does hitting a magnet do to its magnetism?
2. Name two ways in which a magnet can lose its magnetism.
3. Draw a diagram showing how you would store two bar magnets.

MAGNETIC COMPASSES

The earth is magnetic. This fact has been known for centuries. One of the most important properties of a magnet is that if it is suspended (hung) and allowed to turn freely, it will point toward the earth's magnetic north pole. A suspended magnet is called a magnetic compass. It is essential for certain long journeys, such as sailing on the ocean away from landmarks. By knowing in which direction the magnetic north pole is, people can calculate in which direction they are going. This enables them to go in a straight line rather than to wander around in circles.

From earliest times, sailors suspended a piece of lodestone (see page 6) to make a compass. The end of the lodestone that pointed to the earth's magnetic north pole was called the north-seeking pole of the magnet, because it always pointed toward the magnetic north pole. This name has been shortened to the north pole of the compass. The other end of the magnet is now called the south pole of the compass.

Magnetic compasses in ships, planes, and cars are usually filled with liquid. The liquid stops the magnetic needle from swinging around too wildly, and allows it to give a constant, accurate reading. These floating compasses have been used since the early fifteenth century.

Compasses have to be kept far away from iron, so that the magnetic field is not disturbed. Many old compasses had cases made of wood and brass. Inside the case the magnet could swing freely.

Above A diagram of the earth's magnetic field. The poles are where the field lines are closest together.

Left An old compass. Its box is made from nonmagnetic materials, so that its performance is not spoiled.

ACTIVITY

MAKING A MAGNETIC COMPASS

YOU NEED

- **a strong bar magnet**
- **cellophane tape**
- **thread**
- **a strong cardboard box**
- **scissors**

1 Make a tape sling to hold the bar magnet.
2 Place the magnet in the middle of the sling.
3 Press the tape to hold the magnet.
4 Make two holes in the sling.
5 Pass a length of thread through both holes.
6 Hang the magnet up by the thread.

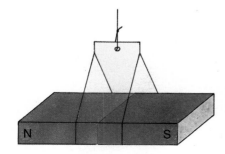

7 Which way does the magnet point?
8 Push the magnet and wait for it to settle. What happens?

9 Cut the base from a cardboard box.
10 Stand the box on end and make a small hole in the middle at the top.
11 Hold your magnet in its sling by a thread and push the thread through the hole in the box.

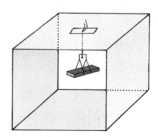

12 Tape the thread to the box. See that the magnet hangs freely.
13 Turn the box so that the magnet points through the openings.
14 Find out which end of the magnet points north.
15 Mark this compass point on the top of the box.
16 Mark the other compass points.

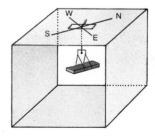

17 Take your compass to your school playground.
18 Walk north. Go as far as your school boundary.

TEST YOURSELF

1. What does a magnetic compass do?
2. Why is a magnetic compass useful for a journey?
3. Draw the four main compass points.

THE EARTH AS A MAGNET

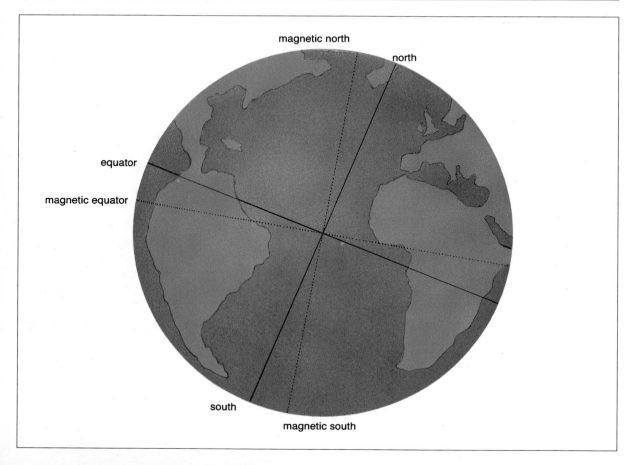

You have already learned that the earth is a large magnet. It is as if the earth has a bar magnet inside it. This bar magnet would have one end at the magnetic north pole and the other end at the magnetic south pole. If the earth is a magnet, then it must be surrounded by a magnetic field. This causes all compasses to point to the earth's magnetic north pole.

The earth also has a geographical north pole, which is in the Arctic Circle. The geographical north pole is the point around which the earth rotates. In the northern hemisphere (the sky north of the equator), the North Star shines almost directly over the geographical north pole. It is the only star in the sky that appears not to move. Because the North Star appears "fixed" it has been used by navigators for centuries to find the north.

At the moment, the magnetic north pole is in northern Canada. If you look at a globe of the earth, you will see that the magnetic north pole is about 1200 miles south of the geographical north pole.

All the lines of longitude on a map join the geographical north and south poles. So a compass pointing to the magnetic north pole points slightly to one side of the lines of longitude.

ACTIVITIES

MAKING A FLOATING COMPASS

YOU NEED

- **a wooden block**
- **a hammer**
- **a small nail**
- **a large jar with plastic lid**
- **thread**
- **a horseshoe magnet**
- **a plastic button**

WARNING: Be very careful when using a hammer.

1 Using the block as a support, hammer a nail through the center of the lid to make a hole.
2 Tie a length of thread to the middle of the horseshoe magnet.
3 Push the thread up through the underside of the lid and tie the end to the plastic button.

4 Check that the magnet hangs down and turns freely.
5 Fill the jar with water and replace the lid.
6 Find which end of the magnet points north. Mark the compass points on the lid.

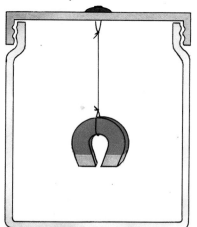

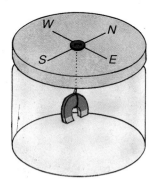

7 Use your compass on a journey. Compare it with the compass you made on page 23.

FINDING THE NORTH POLE

YOU NEED

- **a large globe of the earth**

1 Find the geographical north and south poles on your globe.
2 Turn the globe slowly. Note how the lines of longitude are marked.
3 Find the magnetic north pole.
4 Note how far it is from the geographical north pole.

TEST YOURSELF

1. Which star did navigators use to plot a course?
2. Why are some compasses filled with liquid?
3. Where do you find the magnetic north pole?

ATTRACTION AND REPULSION

A magnetic levitation train (Maglev) on a test run in Japan. There are two strong magnetic fields: one on the train and one on the track. These fields repel each other, so the train floats above the track.

Magnets and magnetic needles of compasses show magnetic attraction and repulsion. The north-seeking pole is attracted to the earth's magnetic north pole and repelled (pushed away) from the earth's magnetic south pole.

The attraction and repulsion seems to be different between two magnets. The north pole of one magnet will be strongly attracted to the south pole of another magnet. If you bring together two north poles or two south poles the magnets repel each other. The rule for magnets is "like poles repel and unlike poles attract."

We now know that the north pole of a magnet cannot possibly be attracted to another north pole, not even the earth's magnetic north pole. The poles of a magnet are, in fact, the opposite of their names. The confusion arose years ago when the north-seeking pole of a compass, which is attracted to the earth's magnetic pole, had its name shortened to "north pole."

ACTIVITY

YOU NEED

- **cellophane tape**
- **2 strong bar magnets, with north and south poles marked**
- **string**

1 Make a tape sling to hold one of the bar magnets (see page 23).
2 Hang the sling from a piece of string. You can suspend it from the edge of a wooden table or get a friend to hold it.
3 Wait until the sling is steady.
4 Bring the south pole of the second bar magnet up to the north pole of the hanging magnet. What happens?

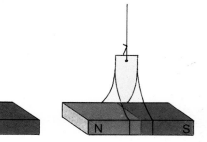

5 Bring the north pole of the second bar magnet up to the north pole of the hanging magnet. What happens?

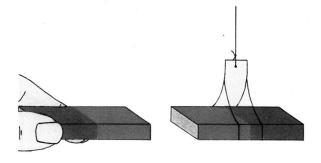

6 Repeat the experiment using the south pole of the hanging magnet.

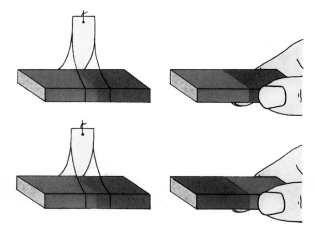

7 What is the pattern in your results?

TEST YOURSELF

1. What happens when the north pole of a magnet is placed near
   - the north pole of another magnet?
   - the south pole of another magnet?
2. What is the rule about the attraction and repulsion of the magnetic poles of magnets?
3. Explain why the north pole of a magnetic compass needle points toward the earth's magnetic north pole.

MORE USES FOR MAGNETS

An electromagnet being used in a scrap yard. It sorts heavy, magnetic objects from the waste, and lifts them up and away.

A suspended magnet, or magnetic compass, is a very useful instrument and can be used for different tasks. Magnets attract magnetic materials, such as iron and nickel, and so a magnetized compass needle will move toward them even if they are hidden or buried. For example, a magnetic compass can be used to detect iron pipes hidden below ground or within walls. The magnetic needle will point toward the iron pipes instead of pointing toward the magnetic north pole. A compass can also detect iron ore buried underground, to see if there are sufficient quantities for mining. It can also be used to detect whether or not a piece of iron is magnetized.

Magnets can also be used for sorting. A compass can be used to sort magnetic from nonmagnetic materials. This is very useful for sorting metals in scrap yards, since most metals are nonmagnetic.

The main use of a magnetic compass, however, is finding direction, because it always points to the magnetic north pole.

1 Put the liquid into the glass jar.
2 Stir the iron filings into the liquid.
3 Tie string to the plastic bag so that you can lower the magnet into the liquid.

4 When the magnet is in the liquid, what happens to the iron filings?
5 Draw what you see, showing the pattern of the lines of force.
6 What happens if you bring another magnet to the side of the jar?

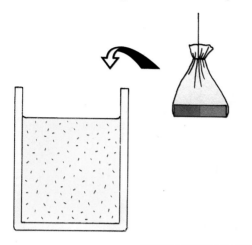

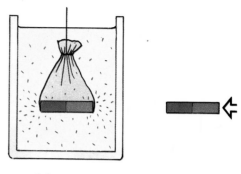

7 Draw this pattern.

MAGNETIC FIELD PATTERNS

YOU NEED

- **a salt shaker**
- **iron filings**
- **a sheet of thin cardboard**
- **2 books**
- **2 bar magnets**

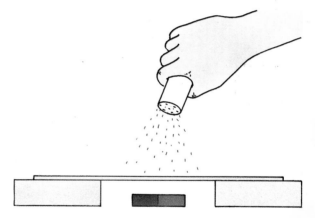

1 Half fill the salt shaker with iron filings.
2 Place the sheet of cardboard on two books to make a bridge.
3 Put a bar magnet under the bridge. Sprinkle iron filings onto the sheet of cardboard. Gently tap the cardboard.

4 Make a drawing of the lines of force.
5 Put two bar magnets under the cardboard, north to south pole.
6 Draw the pattern of the opposite poles of the magnets attracting each other.

TEST YOURSELF

1. Are magnetic field lines closest in the middle or at the ends of a bar magnet?
2. Magnetic field lines show the . . . . and . . . . of the magnetic force.
3. Why do iron filings form a pattern around a magnet?

PLOTTING MAGNETIC FIELDS

You have already seen that a magnetic field can be shown using iron filings. However, this is not very accurate. A better method is to use small compasses called plotting compasses. Here, the compass needle is a permanent magnet, and will be attracted to another magnet in a certain way. The needle on the compass will line up along a line of force. If you move a compass around a magnet and carefully mark the position of the compass needle each time, you will make a drawing of the magnetic lines of force around the magnet (do not forget that these lines do not really exist).

In the previous chapter, you tried the iron filings activity with two bar magnets placed end to end, north to south poles. The lines of force were very close together, because the two attracting fields joined their forces.

Now, if two bar magnets are placed together with their similar poles facing each other, there is a repulsion between the magnets. The lines of force leaving the ends of the magnets are pushed away from each other, leaving a space where there are no magnetic lines of force, because there is no attraction.

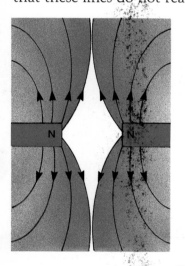 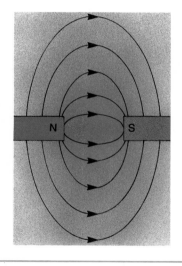

Diagrams to show the lines of magnetic field force when two magnets attract each other (right) and repel each other (left).

ACTIVITIES

MAGNETIC FIELD PATTERNS

YOU NEED

- **a sheet of thin cardboard**
- **2 books**
- **2 bar magnets**
- **a sheet of paper**
- **cellophane tape**
- **a small plotting compass**

1 Place the sheet of cardboard on two books to make a bridge. Put a bar magnet under the bridge.

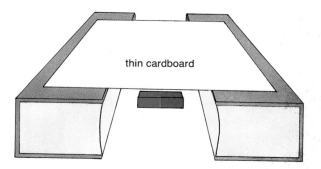

thin cardboard

2 Tape the paper on the cardboard.
3 Place your plotting compass on the paper at the end of the magnet.
4 Put pencil dots on the paper showing the position of the north and south poles of the compass needle.

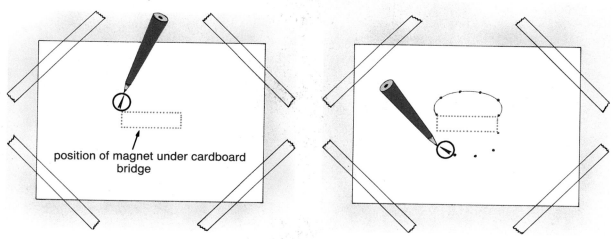

position of magnet under cardboard bridge

5 Move the compass to the next position. Mark two more dots.
6 Repeat this until you have created a dot pattern. Carefully join up the dots. Look at your iron filings results.

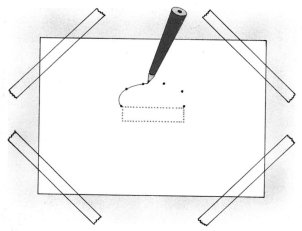

7 Repeat this, starting at the other side of the magnet, and in different places along the magnet.

TEST YOURSELF

1. Draw the lines of force between similar poles of a magnet.
2. Describe how a magnetic compass can be used to show the lines of force around a bar magnet.

RECORDING TAPE

A robot selecting computer reel tapes. The tape is coated in magnetic material, which is used to store information.

You probably have a machine that you use to play your favorite music. There are different kinds, but a very common one is a tape recorder, which plays audio cassettes.

Inside an audio cassette is a long strip of tape. The tape has particles of magnetic material scattered throughout the film on its surface. The particles can be moved into patterns by a small, powerful magnet. On blank tape, the particles form no pattern.

When a recording is to be made, sound waves from a human voice, or musical instruments, enter a microphone. This converts the sound waves into electrical waves. These can then be used to move a small, powerful magnet. The magnet rearranges the particles on the recording tape to form the exact pattern of the electrical waves. When you want to hear the recording, you put the cassette tape in the cassette player.

The pattern on the tape is read and converted back into electrical waves. These waves go to a loudspeaker, which converts the electrical waves back into sound waves. You then hear the recording that is on the cassette.

Provided that the tape is kept far away from any other magnets, the recording will last a long time. If the tape does get near another magnet, the particles of magnetic material will get pulled out of position and the recording will be ruined.

ACTIVITY

MAGNETIC RECORDING TAPE

YOU NEED

- **a cassette recorder**
- **a bar magnet**
- **a blank cassette tape**
- **a pencil to turn the cassette spool**

1 Record your voice on the cassette tape.
2 Play it back to make sure the machine is working properly.
3 Remove the cassette tape and stroke the tape with one end of the magnet.

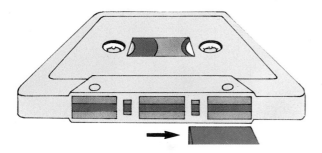

4 Carefully turn the spool with the pencil and stroke all the tape as you turn, back to the beginning.

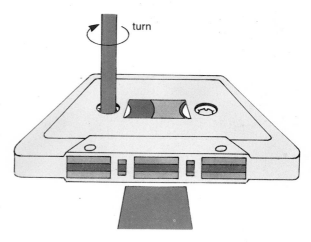

turn

5 Replace the tape in the machine.
6 Play it back again.
7 What does your tape recording sound like now?
8 Record your voice again over the same place on the tape. Play it back. Is it still a good recording?

REMEMBER: Never store your cassette tapes near any magnets.

TEST YOURSELF

1. How does a microphone record sound waves?
2. Why is a cassette tape covered with magnetic material?
3. What happens if you stroke a cassette tape with a magnet?

MAGNETISM FROM ELECTRICITY

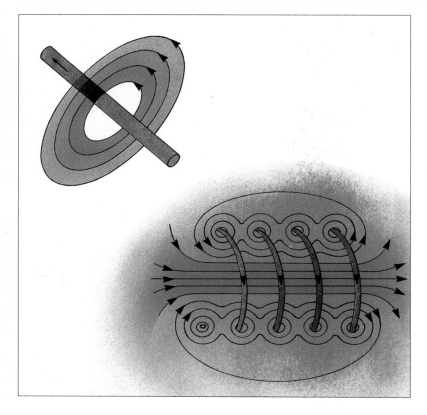

Diagrams to show the magnetic fields around a straight wire (above) and a coiled wire (below). The fields exist only while electricity is running through the wires.

In 1819, the Danish physicist Hans Christian Oersted found that a magnetic field was created when electricity passed through a wire. When electricity flows through a wire, a magnetic field is created around the wire.

If a compass is placed near a copper wire, the needle will not be attracted to the wire because copper is a nonmagnetic metal. If electricity is passed through the wire, a magnetic field is created around the wire. This magnetic field will attract the magnetized needle of the compass. When the electricity is switched off, the magnetic field goes away, and the compass needle returns to its original position. By looking at the compass needle, you can detect when electricity is passing through a wire.

The strength of a magnetic field depends on the amount of electricity (the current) passing through the wire. If the current is weak, the magnetic field will be weak and may be difficult to detect even with a sensitive magnetized needle of a compass.

The magnetic effect can be increased if the wire is coiled around the compass. Each turn of the coil creates a magnetic field, so coiling increases the effect. The more turns in the coil, the greater the magnetic effect and the more the needle moves. In the 1700s the Italian scientist Galvani discovered this effect and used it to invent an electrical detector called a galvanometer. This contains a coil of wire around a magnetic compass. The compass turns to show how much current there is in the wire.

ACTIVITY

YOU NEED

- **insulated copper wire**
- **a 6V battery**
- **a switch**
- **a magnetic compass**
- **a small cardboard or plastic box, to fit the compass**

1 Make a circuit using the battery, copper wire, and the switch.
2 Remove the insulation from the ends of the wire. Tighten all connections.

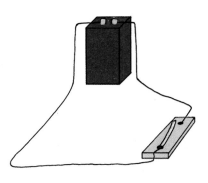

3 Place the compass on the wire. Check that the compass needle points north.

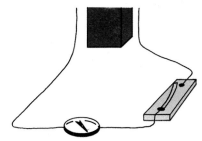

4 Move the wire so that it is north-south, in line with the needle.

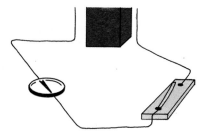

5 Press the switch on and off. What happens to the compass needle when electricity flows along the wire?
6 What happens when you switch off?

7 Connect the battery the other way around. Switch on. What happens?
8 Place the compass in the small box.
9 Wind the copper wire 10 times around the box.

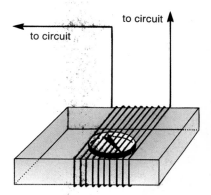

to circuit

to circuit

10 Connect the circuit as before. Press the switch on and off.
11 Does the compass needle move more?
12 Wind the copper wire 20 times around the box. Switch the current on and off.
13 Does the compass needle move more than when there were only 10 turns of wire?

TEST YOURSELF

1. Who first discovered that a magnetic field is created when electricity passes through a wire?
2. Describe how you would prove that a magnetic field is created when electricity passes through the wire.
3. How does a galvanometer work?

ELECTROMAGNETS AT WORK

The magnetic field made around a wire when an electric current flows through it can be useful. Putting a piece of magnetic material in a magnetic field causes the material to become a temporary magnet. This is the way in which an electromagnet is made. An electromagnet is an iron bar surrounded by a coil of wire, through which a current flows, making the iron bar into a temporary magnet. When the current is switched off, the magnetic field disappears and the iron is no longer magnetic.

Electromagnets can be more convenient than permanent magnets. An electromagnet works only when electricity flows through the wire, so you can switch the magnetism off and on, as you could an electric light.

Doorbell

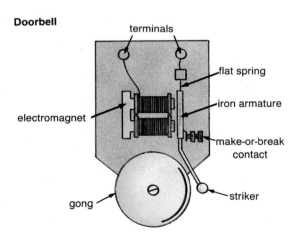

You probably have an electric doorbell which contains an electromagnet. When someone pushes the button by the door, electricity flows through the wire coil and makes the electromagnet work. The iron armature is pulled toward the magnet, which breaks the contact. This switches off the electromagnet. The armature springs back, making the contact again, so that the whole process is repeated very rapidly.

The gong is struck when the armature is attracted to the electromagnet. If the make-or-break contact is properly adjusted, the bell will ring smoothly.

Another familiar piece of equipment that uses an electromagnet is the telephone. When you speak into a telephone mouthpiece, the sound waves push a diaphragm (flat disc). The diaphragm pushes against tiny grains of carbon. These are part of an electric circuit. The more the carbon granules are pushed together, the more electricity flows. The amount of electricity passing corresponds to the sounds you are making. This electricity goes through the telephone wires until it reaches the earpiece of the listener's telephone. The earpiece is a loudspeaker containing an electromagnet. When electricity flows into the electromagnet's coil, the magnetism attracts an iron diaphragm, which moves to create sound waves again. The more the electricity flows, the more the diaphragm moves.

Huge electromagnets are used in junk yards to lift heavy objects made of magnetic materials. They also have many other uses.

Telephone Earpiece

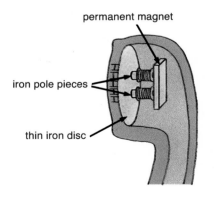

ACTIVITY

MAKING AN ELECTROMAGNET

YOU NEED

- **a large steel nail**
- **a length of covered copper wire**
- **a switch**
- **a 6V battery**
- **a magnetic compass**

1 Use your compass to see if the nail is magnetized.
2 Wind a length of wire 30 times around the nail. Make sure that you wind the wire in the same direction.

3 Connect one end of the wire to the battery.
4 Connect the switch to the other end of the battery terminal.
5 Check that the insulation has been removed from the copper wire when making the circuit.
6 Make all the connections tight.

7 Switch on for one second. Is the nail magnetized? Will the nail pick up magnetic objects? How far will your electromagnet attract a magnetic compass?

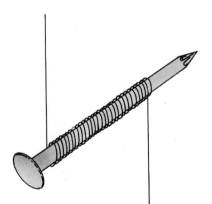

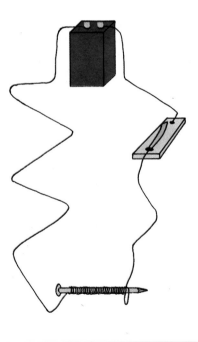

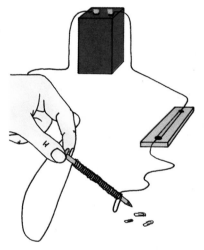

8 What happens if you connect the battery the other way around?
9 What happens if you use 50 turns of wire on the nail?
10 What happens if you use two batteries?

TEST YOURSELF

1. If you were given an electromagnet with 30 turns of wire in its coil, explain how you would attempt to make it a stronger electromagnet.
2. How does an electromagnetic doorbell work?
3. Explain how a telephone works.

ELECTRICITY FROM A MAGNET

If electricity can create a magnetic field, then it should be possible for a magnetic field to create electricity. This idea first came to the British scientist, Michael Faraday, in 1831. He knew, from Oersted's work, that electricity passing through a coil created a magnetic field. So he passed a bar magnet into a coil of wire. This created electricity in the wire. He proved that electricity had been created by using a galvanometer.

Electricity will drive an electric motor. An electric motor is a coil turning between two poles of a permanent magnet. The more electricity passing into the coil, the faster the coil turns. If the electricity is switched off, the coil stops turning and the motor stops.

If you mechanically turn a coil of wire between the poles of a magnet, electricity will be created in the wires of the coil. An electric motor used to create electricity in this way is called a dynamo.

Dynamos are used to create electricity for our homes. These dynamos are turned by turbines. The turbines are turned by jets of steam. The steam is made by heated water. The water is heated by burning oil or coal, or by using nuclear power. The turbine can also be turned by water, as in a water wheel, or by a windmill. In each system, large coils of wire are turned between magnets to create electricity.

Left *A simple d.c. motor.*

Below *An a.c. generator (dynamo). The coil is turned mechanically between the poles of the magnet, thus creating an a.c. current.*

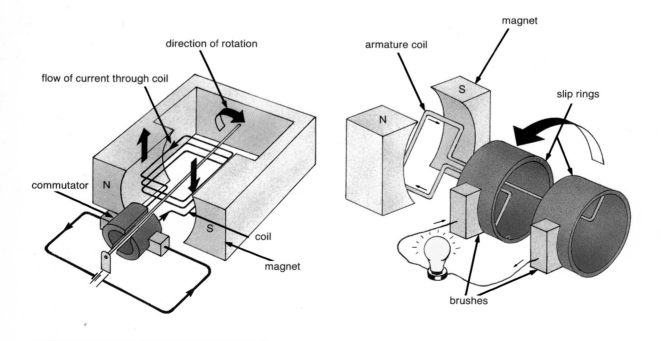

ACTIVITY

FARADAY'S EXPERIMENT TO MAKE ELECTRICITY

YOU NEED

- **a magnetic compass**
- **a cardboard or plastic box**
- **a length of thin covered copper wire**
- **a broom handle**
- **a strong bar magnet**

5 Check also that this 50-turn coil is well away from the compass needle.

6 Slowly put the north pole of your magnet into the 50-turn coil.

1 Put the magnetic compass in the box.
2 Wind 20 turns of wire around the box.
3 Make a large 50-turn coil at the wire's other end by winding it around a broom handle, then removing.

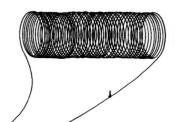

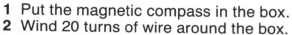

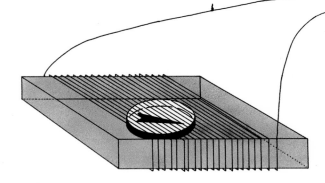

7 What happens to the compass needle? If the needle moves there must be electricity in the wire.

8 Slowly withdraw the magnet. What happens?

9 Slowly put the south pole of your magnet into the coil. Which way does the compass needle move?

10 What happens if you put the south pole of your magnet into the coil from the other direction?

4 Check that this coil is large enough for a bar magnet to pass through it.

11 How could you make a stronger electrical current?

TEST YOURSELF

1. Who was the first person to make electricity from a magnet?
2. What does a dynamo do?
3. How is electricity made for our homes?

TRANSFORMERS

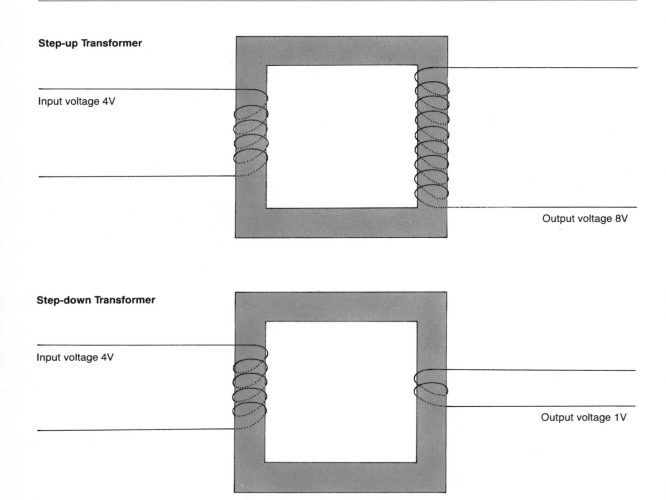

Step-up Transformer

Input voltage 4V

Output voltage 8V

Step-down Transformer

Input voltage 4V

Output voltage 1V

The electricity supply to your home is always at the same voltage. It is much lower than the voltage in the nation's electricity network. This is higher than we need, because it is more economical. To reduce this voltage to the level that is needed, a device called a transformer is used.

The usual type of transformer has a square loop of iron and two coils of wire. One coil is on one side of the loop and the other coil is on the opposite side. An electric current flows into one coil, causing the iron to become an electromagnet. The magnetism causes electricity to flow in the other coil. If the second coil has fewer turns than the first coil, the voltage going out is decreased (step-down transformer). If the second coil has more turns than the first coil, the voltage going out is increased (step-up transformer).

Transformers can be used to convert voltage to a very low level. Transformers allow some types of toys and appliances to use household current.

ACTIVITY

MAKING A TRANSFORMER

YOU NEED

- **a 6V battery**
- **a magnetic compass in a cardboard or plastic box**
- **a switch**
- **a long, steel nail or knitting needle**
- **lengths of insulated copper wire**

1 Make an electromagnet by winding 30 turns of insulated wire around one end of the nail or knitting needle.
2 Connect this coil to a battery and switch. This is your first, or primary, circuit.

3 Wind another length of wire 10 times around a box holding the compass.
4 Use the wire to make a 10-turn coil at the other end of the nail or knitting needle. This is your secondary circuit.

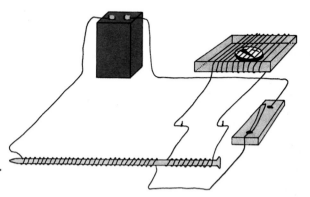

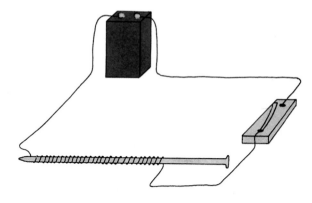

5 Look at your compass needle. Is it moving? Is electricity in either circuit?
6 Switch on the electricity in the primary circuit. Does the compass needle move in the secondary circuit?
7 Is electricity in the secondary circuit?
8 What happens if you use 20 and 30 turns of wire in your secondary circuit?
9 How could you make the electromagnet in your primary circuit stronger?

TEST YOURSELF

1. List two ways of increasing the magnetic power of the electromagnet in the primary circuit of a transformer.
2. How can you increase the amount of electricity formed in the secondary coil of a transformer?
3. How does a transformer work?

Glossary

Alloy A mixture of metals: for example, brass is an alloy of copper and zinc.

Alternating current (a.c.) An electric current that flows first in one direction, then in the opposite. The direction changes at regular intervals.

Armature A soft iron or steel bar that is placed across the poles of an electromagnet. It turns the magnetic force into movement.

Attraction (in magnets) The power of the magnet to pull magnetic materials towards itself.

Battery An electric cell that uses a chemical reaction to make electricity.

Carbon A nonmetallic element that conducts electricity. It is not a magnetic material.

Direct current (d.c.) An electric current that flows in one direction only.

Dynamo A machine that produces electric current by moving a wire coil within a magnetic field.

Electricity A form of energy created by moving electrons. An electron is a tiny, negatively charged particle in an atom.

Electromagnet A magnet made when electricity flows through a coil of wire wrapped around a piece of iron.

Galvanometer A machine for detecting electrical current. It was invented by Luigi Galvani.

Generator A machine for producing electricity.

Geographical north pole The earth rotates around this point, one full turn every day. It is in the Arctic.

Geographical south pole The opposite to the geographical north pole. It is in the Antarctic.

Keeper (in magnets) Small bars, usually made of soft iron, that are used to link the north and south poles of magnets. They keep the magnetism while the magnets are being stored.

Longitude Imaginary lines connecting the geographical north and south poles. They are identified in degrees east or west of a line drawn through Greenwich, England.

Loudspeaker A machine that converts electrical waves into sound waves.

Magnetic field The space around a magnet in which the magnetic force is felt.

Microphone A machine that converts sound waves into electrical waves. The opposite of a loudspeaker.

Ore A rock or mineral containing a metal that is valuable enough to be mined.

Permanent Lasting for a very long time or forever.

Power station A plant for generating electric power by converting other forms of energy into electrical energy.

Repel To push away from. In magnets, it means the effect of two like poles on one another (repulsion).

Sound waves Vibrations or disturbances in the air that cause us to hear.

Steel Iron that has had carbon and other substances added to make it harder.

Temporary Lasting for a short time. The opposite of, permanent.

Transformer An electrical device that is used for changing one voltage to another.

Voltage Electric force. It is what pushes current around a circuit.

Books to Read

The Electromagnetic Spectrum: Key to the Universe, Franklyn M. Branley (Harper & Row Junior Books, 1979)

Electricity and Magnetism, Gregory Vogt (Franklin Watts, 1985)

Picture Acknowledgments

The author and publishers would like to thank the following for allowing illustrations to be reproduced in this book: PHOTRI 6, 12, 20, 30; Science Photo Library *frontispiece,* 10, 16, 22 (below right), 26, 28, 36; ZEFA *cover,* 8, 14, 22 (left). All artwork is by Jenny Hughes.

Index